—Imagine—
Yourself Real

USE THE POWER OF YOUR MIND TO BECOME THE
REAL YOU THAT'S DYING TO GET OUT

In 13 Mental Exercises
& 10 Easy Rules

by

IRENE LAFETRA

Salt of the Earth Press
Springbrook, WI

Imagine Yourself Real:
Use the power of your mind to
become the real you that's dying to get out
by Irene LaFetra

First Edition
Printed in the United States of America
Copyright © 2009 Salt of the Earth Press

ISBN: 0-9816949-3-4
ISBN13: 978-0-9816949-3-1

All rights reserved. No part of this publication may be reproduced or transmitted in any form or by any means, electronic or mechanical, including photocopy, recording or any information or retrieval system, without written permission from Salt of the Earth Press.

Orders and editorial comments may be addressed to Salt of the Earth Press.

Salt of the Earth Press
W4456 Hwy 63
Springbrook, WI 54875
www.saltpress.com

Dedicated to all the real people in my life.

There are certain rare physical, metabolic and psychological disorders that affect appearance and behavior. Those issues require the assistance of a medical consultant such as a family physician. If you suspect you have such a condition, please see your doctor or other health care provider before beginning any lifestyle altering program. However, this program is designed to work in harmony with medical conditions or restrictions and may be used safely under the direction of your physician.

Contents

Beginning *1*

Section One: Who are you, really?
    Until you know who you are, you cannot be yourself. *5*
    Exercise 1: How do others see you? 9
    Exercise 2: Seeing with new eyes 11
    Exercise 3: Who you really are 13
    Exercise 4: Study your role model 17

Section Two: Finding your style
    For lasting happiness, represent yourself honestly
    in your body, mind and soul *21*
    Exercise 5: Design your life 24
    Exercise 6: Refine the design 26
    Exercise 7: Love 28
    Exercise 8: Visualize it! 29

Section Three: Exploring rules
    Even the Universe operates according to Laws *31*
    Exercise 9: Sample rules 34
    Exercise 10: Rules for the new you 36

Section Four: Implementing your new rules for life
    Begin as you mean to go on.
    And if you falter, begin again. *39*
    Exercise 11: Challenges 42
    Exercise 12: Rules for Breaking your rules 44
    Exercise 13: Time for Change 46

There is no Ending *48*

Reference *49*
    List of descriptive words 49
    Your body 51
    Your face 52
    Categorized people 53
    Your role model 54
    The "Real Me" 55
    My Rules 56

Beginning

Are you struggling in your life and find yourself thinking that the people around you, your co-workers, family, friends or the clerk at the convenience store, just don't understand you? Do you feel saddened that those who should know you best, are judging you based upon things over which you have no control like your weight?

Why and how are they losing sight of who you are?

The human mind thinks in images, not words, but words do paint pictures for our minds. Once an image is entered into the subconscious, the mind accepts it as reality. Unfortunately, the mind stores everything it is impressed with and just like your conscious behavior, we are most impressed with emotionally rich, sensory laden images.

As an experiment I want you to read the following comments that many people have heard from others and even from themselves about themselves. Pause after reading each one and see if you can *feel* if it has meaning for you.

>You're fat.
>You are so stupid!
>What a pig.
>You'll never amount to anything.
>Shut up!
>You should be ashamed of yourself.
>You can't do that!
>You don't deserve that.
>No one is going to love you the way you are.

You're an idiot.
What makes you think you can be a _____?
Get over yourself!
Forget about your dreams.
You're nothing, a nobody!

If you felt a twang of pain, it's because the phrase that bugs you has already been stored in your subconscious as an emotionally rich, sensory laden image. Your mind doesn't know that the words may have been spoken in anger or by someone who was crippled by cruelty, or by your own voice when faced with fear, uncertainty or lack of confidence. Idle words, spoken in jest or hate, whether true or lies, even those that are unbelievable, lodge in our minds if they create an emotional response or include sensory details like smells or sensations. The bigger the response, the greater weight our subconscious gives the memory.

Because your mind doesn't know the difference between true statements of fact about you, and these hurtful images of limit, it simply takes it all at face value, assuming the most emotionally charged images are the most powerful and appropriate.

You have been living your life, acting, reacting, and making choices based on the most emotionally charged images you have stored, not the most accurate.

You have defined yourself internally in all areas with a series of rules based upon those images. Your mind has stored definitions for your weight (fat, skinny, just right, muscular), your activity level (lazy, active, athletic, couch-potato), style of dress (sloppy, professional, elegant), occupation (laborer, lawyer, Indian Chief) and even your attitude (happy, melancholy, depressed, cheerful, somber, positive).

You're on auto-pilot!

The next step is for your body to follow the dictates, or rules, of your subconscious mind. You live up to the mind's expectation that you are fat, or stupid, or unworthy and it becomes physical reality which then "proves" the image to your conscious mind, repeating the cycle endlessly.

You can stop the cycle.

This little workbook is all about resetting those subconscious images of yourself using your imagination.
You can use these techniques to change your appearance, your career, your location and most importantly, your attitude by changing the rules.
All the time, everywhere in this universe, people, animals, planets, even the air we breathe, are acting and reacting according to rules. We, as humans, may call some of our rules Religion or Science or "just the way I am."
Without you even realizing it, you have a set of rules that have defined your every fiber. You may have heard them from your parents and adopted them by default, or you may have created them as a defense against the slings and arrows of life. You may even have purposefully constructed a set of rules for yourself that were, at one point in your life, a positive thing but that you have since outgrown.
Rules, as we apply them to our lives, are things of little substance that happen primarily in our minds. We may make concessions for rules that are outside of ourselves, but for the most part they are created, implemented and destroyed within our mind's eye, otherwise known as our imagination.
I was a health care provider in a large metropolitan city for 15 years. I attended the births of about a thousand babies and got to sit in a front row seat to observe the intimate workings of the minds, lives and lifestyles of all those families. Most of my patients were ordinary people like you and me but some were entertainers, writers, dancers, politicians and even prostitutes.
I noticed that the overweight women and the thin and fit women, the successful and the working poor, the abusive and the abused, all made remarks as statements of fact that defined them. In looking at their homes, I saw patterns of behavior that I

was easily able to quantify as directly related to these definitions.

The underlying theme was that these people, the women who complained constantly, and those who seemed to not have a care in the world, the older kids in the families who were lazy, or sullen, or angry, or full of joy and life, and the husbands who had high blood pressure, or beer bellies, or played soccer, or flew jets, all of them, had made rules in their minds and were living according to those rules.

You can apply the exercises in this book to many things in your life, including weight, relationships, and career. In fact, by the end of it, you will probably have changed much different aspects of your life in addition to what you had planned on changing. My hope is that these changes will reflect the internal, authentic you and allow you to live your life wholistically happier.

Give yourself permission to write in the margins, glue pictures on blank spots, and staple paper over pages to add to your notes.

If you want to change your life right now by changing your internal vision of yourself, turn the page. Begin.

Section 1

Who are you?
Until you know who you are, you cannot be yourself.

Who are you?

The Who sings it best, but you are answering this question every moment of every day in every thing you do, think and say.

Some people suffer when they look in the mirror and not see what they feel they look like. It hurts and it makes it hard to face the world in ease and joy. It sometimes might even be hard to be seen by their own family. It could be their weight, or some other appearance issue that is creating an intense and negative focus.

Others might be hitting a brick wall of atttude. No matter how hard they try, they can't convince their employer to see their potential.

You may find that you have a similar issue in another area.

The problem is that your image of who and what you are doesn't align with your appearance or behavior, which conveys preconceived notions our society or family has about people who look and act just like you.

By aligning who you really are on the inside with how that true self is reflected in actions, behaviors and preferences, your outer appearance will be altered.

This book will help you see yourself as others see you. You will break through the image you have of yourself and see yourself with new eyes. You will also create a vision of how you *should* look and live, based on who you really are. Then, you'll study how people who are similar to your inner self, look on the outside, and how they act, eat and live. At that point, you can begin designing a set of rules to live by that will enable you to align your behavior and appearance with who you are.

Lastly, I've included a set of charts, and other reference

material to help you in finding a perfect fit of behaviors and tools, conditions and rules.

This isn't hard. Have fun in this place of discovery, and dive in.

Exercise 1: How do others see you?

By examining how you believe others view you, you will gain insight into the false image you may be projecting to the world. The next page includes a series of observations that you will label with descriptive words you believe others apply to you.

It might be very difficult for you to pick yourself apart this way depending upon who you are and how much baggage you carry in your life about your personality and appearance. I suggest you go somewhere quiet and private to do this first part of the exercise.

It is normal and natural for a person to play back old mental recordings. If your parents told you that you were stupid, you may automatically write down that everyone thinks you're stupid, even though you now have a PhD and have earned the respect of many people that you and society view as intelligent. Think about each word you use to describe yourself. Try to be honest.

There will be cases where someone has told you that you are a particular way. Usually this is done as an insult, or as a way to manipulate you into certain behaviors or processes. If that description is not repeated in any other relationships, or perhaps only appears in certain relationships, then you need to examine it closely.

For example, what if your spouse tells you in words or reaction that you are messy and lazy. However, your boss at work thinks you're a meticulous, hard worker as do the folks at church and your parents. This is an area to examine. Sometimes we are one way with one person and another way in every other area of our lives. Trying to categorize those different possibilities is hard, but if you try you may gain a real insight into who you are. Make notes about those observations. If you need more space, write on one of the blank pages and refer to that page number in the space.

When you're done, you should have a list of words that are how you *think* people see you. How they really see you may be quite different so in actuality, this list is your perception or reflection of how you think people see you. It is doubtful that you could find someone who would actually give you an honest appraisal, or that you would believe them.

If you get stumped for what words to use, I've included a list of words, good, bad, flattering and hurtful, on page 46. The words you use only have to resonate truth with you. They don't have to match any other ideal. For instance, under "gender" you may put "masculine" or you might write "man" or perhaps "boy" would feel more appropriate. Use words that *feel* like truth.

How people see me:

Gender _____
Age _____
Sexuality _____
Mental and Emotional- over all _____
    Happiness _____
    Intelligence _____
Appearance and Physical- over all _____
    Activity level _____
    Hair color _____
    Hair style _____
    Face - expression _____
    Face - grooming _____
    Face - enhancements (like makeup or piercings) _____
    Body type (muscular, athletic, lazy, etc) _____
    Body size _____
    Cleanliness _____
    Hands - grooming _____
    Feet - grooming _____
    Clothes Style _____
    Clothes colors _____
Lifestyle - over all _____
    Exterior House/Home _____
    Yard or outdoor space _____
    Inside home _____
    Vehicle _____
    Occupation _____
    Education _____
    Recreation _____
Goals _____
_____

Exercise 2: Seeing with new eyes

It's very difficult for anyone to really know what they look like. When we look in the mirror our eyes are naturally attracted to certain spots that either please us or repel us. The teenager may observe his reflection and only see the pimple on his nose, completely missing his muscled arms or long eyelashes. The following exercise may help in making an objective, or as objective as anyone can be about herself, appraisal of appearance.

Find a recent full body photograph of yourself. If you can't find one, set up a digital camera to take a timed photo and snap your picture. Wear whatever you feel comfortable in. Some might prefer this photo be nude and some might want to dress up in their going-to-meeting clothes. It makes no difference. If you have long hair, pull it up or out of the way so that it isn't laying on your shoulders or back. Pick a neutral background like a wall with no pictures on it.

Cut out the picture and paste it on page 48.

Go through magazines or pictures online and look for a photo of the head of a person of your gender and about your age that is the same size as your head in your photo. If you found a picture online you can adjust it's size in an art program. The head you choose should be someone you find reasonably attractive so that it isn't too distracting. This doesn't have to represent how you wish you look. It is just so that you can fool your brain. Carefully cut out that head and paste it on the picture of your body, right over your head.

This exercise is only to allow you to see parts of your body with a fresh persepective. It's normal to zoom into only certain areas, good or bad, and blank out others. This exercise will often shake up your view of yourself.

You might have a very strong reaction to seeing your body with new eyes, or it may not affect you at all. What is your first response? Write down those impressions on the next page. If you need more space, you can write on another piece of paper and tape it over page 12.

_____
_____
_____
_____
_____
_____
_____
_____
_____
_____

Look at the answers you wrote down in Exercise 1. Are they still valid or do you need to refine them? Looking at your body with someone else's face may help you see yourself objectively. You may discover that you aren't as overweight as you thought, or that your clothes convey a false message or that your posture reflects an inner sorrow. Our non-verbal communication through body language, and physical lifestyle expressions is more powerful that the words we conciously choose to speak to others.

Now find a body that is fit, reasonably attractive and that is also about your age. A good place to find full body photographs of attractive people is the celebrity pages of gossip magazines during Emmy or Oscar Awards. The stars arrive, pose, get photographed, and move on. Do this exercise with your face on that body on page 49, and write your first response to your face on another body below.

_____
_____
_____
_____
_____
_____
_____
_____

Exercise 3: Who you really are

For this exercise you'll be filling in a chart on the next pages.

Block 1: Write down traits or descriptive words that describe who you think you really are for that category. Even if you seldom show these parts of you to others, or even if no one else would agree with you. You *do* know yourself best and though you may not be able to express your true personality that doesn't make it any less true.

Block 2: For each trait or descriptive word, write down how that personality trait equates to appearance, or what it "looks like." A bubbly person might always be smiling. A mothering person might hug everyone all the time and have a large bosom and carry cookies. Even if you don't or can't express the traits you possess, write down how they are displayed in most people.

Block 3: Make a check mark next to the traits you like, that are positive, that present a positive vision, or that serve you well. In other words, put a check next to the traits you want to keep. Put an X next to the traits you would like to be rid of, control or somehow contain. Probably all they need is to be redirected.

Block 4 (second line): Think of people you know, or characters in television shows or movies, who embody these same traits. Jot down their names. James Dean may embody your bad boy image while Jimmy Stewart may be the somewhat confused persona you hate. It doesn't matter who they are, and you don't need to think too much about this. You may, if your knowledge of TV or movies is very limited, use people you know, or people in the news. Don't use characters in books for this exercise since it's very important that you form a visual reference for each trait.

Block 5: Put a P for positive or an N for negative next to each line. There may be some overtly negative traits that serve you well and that you wish to keep and there may be some positive traits that are your downfall that you would love to lose.

You may want to change some of your checks and X's at this point.

How I really am:

1: Real self	2: Looks like	3
4: Example Person		5

Example — What you see yourself being and doing		
Occupation ↓ Key traits that others would see ↓		
1: graphic artist & designer	2: enthusiastic, colorful clothes	3 ✓
4: Mary Englebreit		5 P

Gender
1:	2:	3
4:		5

Age
1:	2:	3
4:		5

Sexuality
1:	2:	3
4:		5

Mental and Emotional- over all
1:	2:	3
4:		5

Happiness
1:	2:	3
4:		5

Intelligence
1:	2:	3
4:		5

Appearance and Physical - over all
1:	2:	3
4:		5

Activity level
1:	2:	3
4:		5

Hair color
1:	2:	3
4:		5

Hair style
1:	2:	3
4:		5

Face - expression

1:	2:	3
4:		5

Face - grooming

1:	2:	3
4:		5

Face - enhancements (like makeup or piercings)

1:	2:	3
4:		5

Body type (muscular, athletic, lazy, etc)

1:	2:	3
4:		5

Body size

1:	2:	3
4:		5

Cleanliness

1:	2:	3
4:		5

Hands - grooming

1:	2:	3
4:		5

Feet - grooming

1:	2:	3
4:		5

Clothes Style

1:	2:	3
4:		5

Clothes colors

1:	2:	3
4:		5

Lifestyle - over all

1:	2:	3
4:		5

Exterior House/Home

1	2:	3
4:		5

Yard or outdoor space

1:	2:	3:
4:		5:

Inside home

1:	2:	3:
4:		5:

Vehicle

1:	2:	3:
4:		5:

Occupation

1:	2:	3:
4:		5:

Education

1:	2:	3:
4:		5:

Recreation

1:	2:	3:
4:		5:

Goals

1:	2:	3:
4:		5:

Exercise 4: Study Your Role Model

You've assessed yourself pretty well. You've identified how others view you, and you've examined your personality and seen it in the context of someone else's life. Now you need to pull it together to see the whole person of whom you really are.

Out of all the people you've listed for the various traits you identified about yourself in Block 4, is there one that really seems to embody who you are? You're looking for someone who is like the real you, including how you should look to reflect your true self. You may wish you were more like a certain person, but think carefully about whether or not you really are like that person. You may want to be like her, but if you aren't like her, and you want to keep the traits of yours that are counter to hers, then you can admire her from afar while patterning yourself after someone more like who you really are.

You might be tempted to choose several people. This isn't a good idea because your mind will form a visual image of the composite person and if there are conflicting attributes, your mind won't be able to firm up this internal vision. If you feel you can't embody your true self in the guise of one person, choose just one aspect of your personality and work on that. Most people choose physical appearance or career in this case and work on other expressions of personality later.

Who you chose: _____

Now you're going to study that person. This is why I wanted you to choose someone who is well known, a character in a movie, or in your real world sphere.

Fill out the following chart about the role model you chose. This might take awhile, and you will probably have to do some Internet or library searches unless the person you chose is someone you know. If it is someone you know, don't tell him or her what you're doing since you'll make them self-conscious and that will skew your observations. If this is a well-known person, I recommend cutting out photos to represent these different observations and gluing them onto page 51. Laughing, angry, working, and candid observations are usually easily found for celebrities.

Although to you it may look like this person has the perfect life, in reality he or she is a person just like you and subject to the same ability to screw up and generally make really stupid choices. Keep that in mind while you're making your observations.

What is it about them that embodies who you really are? _____

_____
_____
_____
_____

What is their body type? _____

_____
_____
_____

Activity level _____

_____

What they do for exercise _____

_____

How do they wear their hair? _____

_____
_____

When they are being casual, what do they look like? _____

_____
_____

When they are dressed up, what do they look like? _____

_____

What do they do for fun? _____

___ Pay attention to how they hold themselves, laugh, pose for photos. These things are physical manifestations of their personality. If the behavior doesn't match what you believed this person to be like, or if you find that it doesn't reflect your ideal and inner self, you may need to switch to another role model. Add more notes about your role model below.

Section 2

Finding Your Style
For lasting happiness, represent yourself honestly
in your body, mind and soul

Finding your style

You know how you should look to reflect who you are, in body, dress and behavior. You can see yourself in your mind's eye. You have photos to help you when the image falters and you have identified the traits about yourself that you really like and want to foster. At this point you may want to spend some time imagining you – the *real* you – living in the life you have, at the job you have, with the friends you have.

Imagine the vision of yourself that you have created going to work, eating out with friends, and participating in your leisure activities.

It looks pretty great, doesn't it? There you are, hair swept back (or up or spiked or whatever) nibbling on canapés at the neighborhood bar with your old buddy Hank from the factory. Okay, so maybe they don't serve canapés at the neighborhood bar and you're actually munching Cheetos, but you get the drift. Imagine it. Feel it. In this section, you will also create tools so that you can see it.

Exercise 5: Design Your Life

Now let's find your lifestyle. You're going to design your life to fit who you really are. You'll want to refer back to Exercise 3 while you fill out these responses. These answers are not how you live your life right now but how your real self, your true personality would live. Some of the answers may not be realistic or even possible for you right now, but don't let that stop you. The purpose of this exercise is to identify the lifestyle that fits your true self. Have fun!

I wake up at _____ because _____
_____

(I have to go to work at 6 am or I like to watch the sunrise, or I stayed up late the night before, or my kids need breakfast and I like to kiss my husband goodbye)

I eat breakfast at _____ and it consists of _____
_____

I spend my day (doing what?) _____
_____

I eat lunch at _____ and it consists of _____
_____

In the evening I (activities or behavior) _____
_____
_____

I eat my evening meal at _____ and it consists of ___
_____

For beverages I drink _____
_____

When I am eating out in public and someone whose opinions matters sees me, I want them to see me eating _____
_____
_____

For a night out I _____

_____

For exercise I _____

_____

For recreation I _____

_____

When I act silly I act like this _____

_____

When I am serious I act like this _____

_____

When I am sad I act like this _____

_____

When I am angry I act like this _____

_____

When I am happy I act like this _____

_____

I am working toward the goal of _____
_____
_____
_____
_____
_____

Exercise 6: Refine the Design

Compare Exercise 1 and Exercise 5. How does the way you live your life right now, differ from the way you would live your life if you were being true to yourself? If right now you eat a diet that is primarily unhealthy but you see yourself as being very concious of what you eat, that's a real dichotomy. If you are really healthy at heart, why are you eating an unhealthy diet? And if you see yourself as having a huge appetite, have you also adjusted your vision for yourself to include being very overweight, because that is a natural consequence of overeating if you aren't an athlete.

Go back and read over your responses. Look for common areas and areas that are in complete contrast. This is a soul-searching exercise. You need to look at yourself, your appearance, and your lifestyle objectively to be able to identify how you can live up to your potential in a new life and body that you have designed.

To be clear on the vision you're constructing you have to be honest and clear in your answers. Dig a little deeper and define your real self a little more. Again, these answers should reflect who your inner self is, not necessarily how you act right now.

1. I get about _____ hours of sleep each night.

2. I spend _____ hours at home and _____ hours at work each day.

3. I spend _____ hours with friends each _____ (day, week, month, etc)

4. The food I eat is primarily _____ (balanced, vegetarian, vegan, soup, etc.)

5. I spend _____ hours each _____ in the following

activity for my career: _____

　　and I wear _____

　　while engaged in that activity.

6.　I spend _____ hours each _____ in the following physical activity: _____

　　and I wear _____

　　while engaged in that activity.

7.　I spend _____ hours each _____ in the following leisure activity: _____

　　and I wear _____

　　while engaged in that activity.

8.　When I am at home relaxing I wear _____.

9. The most admiring thing anyone says about me is (go for broke here – this is your vision) _____
_____
_____
_____
_____
_____
_____
_____
_____

Exercise 7: Love

You may notice that I don't include references to spouses or love interests on these exercises. The reason is that I firmly believe that you have to love you before anyone else will love you to your satisfaction. That means that while there may be many people who love you, you won't be able to accept their love, or you will actually reject their love as not the type of love you want or need, until you allow yourself to be the real you that has been hidden behind your fears, insecurities, cruel history and anger.

This exercise is to illustrate that appearance and behavior have very little to do with one's ability to have a seemingly happy, healthy relationship.

Go to a mall, a large store like Wal-Mart, the grocery store on coupon day, or a church. In other words, go to a crowded place where there are lots of people. Find a place to sit and watch. Notice the people who seem to be happily married or in love. Pay attention to what the partners in those couples look like. Not everyone is beautiful, thin, and well-dressed, no matter what definition you have for those things. Although people are usually initially attracted to one another by looks, they stay together for other reasons. And what constitutes good looks to a potential mate might completely overlook size or hair color or wrinkles.

Work on you, making you happy, creating a life that reflects who you are so that you are in love with yourself. Only then will the complimentary partner for your life be attracted to you. How could someone who was attracted to this false image of you be the person who will compliment the real you?

Exercise 8: Visualize it!

Every thing about the life you have just defined should feel right. From the food you eat to the amount of sleep you get. Go back and change things as you get a clearer vision of who you really are.

Remember the exercise where you cut out a picture of a head and glued it on the picture of your body? This time I want you to find a body that looks close to the way you feel your real self looks. Go shopping for a visual reference for the way you feel your real self looks when you express yourself honestly. Refer to the exercises you have done and remove your emotions from applying preconceived ideas of how you look. When you have found a picture of a body that matches the expression of the traits you defined in exercises 5 and 6 glue your face picture on that body. You may include your hair, or you may wish to just cut out your face and put it over the face on the picture. This could take a few tries until you find the right body, hair and view of your face. You may find several photos of your target vision in various activities that you can use to create many views of yourself. Glue this on page 52. If you need more space, tape or staple at the top another sheet of paper right over page 50 and glue away.

By now we have a vision of what you look like as a reflection of who you are on the inside, and a vision of how your life works, including your lifestyle. This exercise is in your head. From now on you will spend 1 minute 3 times a day visualizing this vision of your life. Turn to Exercise 6 if you need to be reminded of the details and imagine looking like that picture, engaging in those activities, eating those foods.

In your visualization, look outside of your own eyes to see the world. You don't want to be a fly on the wall looking at yourself, you want to experience the real you, in your real body, living your real life. The real life that defines the true you that has, up to now, been hidden.

In the morning you may imagine yourself waking up, taking a shower, seeing your trim and healthy body in the full-length mirror, and eating an apple on your way out the door to play tennis.

At noon, you may visualize yourself shaking hands with your employer after a satisfactory meeting, striding down the street from your office, feeling successful in clothes that attract admiring glances, and happily greeting people who know you.

In the evening, before you go to sleep, you could imagine yourself out on a date with a great new love interest, or hosting a party at your house, or running a marathon and crossing the finish line to the cheers of your family. But look out through your eyes at the world from the body that reflects your true self.

What sort of car would your true self drive? Imagine yourself behind the wheel. What kinds of friends compliment the person you really are? See them and listen in on those conversations. Start living the life that is inside you, dying to get out, now in your visualizations.

Section 3

Exploring Rules

Even the Universe operates according to Laws

Exploring rules

Everyone has rules for life. Vegetarians have a rule to not eat meat. Marathon runners might have a rule that they must run every day no matter what. People who belong to certain religions have rules about worship or other rites within their affiliation. There are rules about how to set the table and rules about how to put the roll of toilet paper on the holder. Even holidays are celebrated according to rules. Laws are rules that have been formalized. Once you have followed a rule long enough it becomes a habit and habits require no thought. Good or bad, the rules are so ingrained that we mindlessly follow them.

Unfortunately we have come to view rules as something bad or restricting. Actually, they give us a framework within which to operate safely and acceptably. Without rules, many of us have become out of control, and have suffered because of it.

Exercise 9: Sample Rules

Think about rules that govern your life and the lives of those you know, either in your family, place of work or community. The categories that follow include some examples of rules that others, including clients of mine, have had. You may believe that some of them are foolish, too restrictive, or too lenient. You may be disgusted or feel that a few are immoral or in some way unacceptable. However you view them, accept that they are the working rules that make others' lives easier, simpler, safer, or in some way rewarding. Add to these categories from rules in your own life or the lives of those you know.

You can see that we all have rules for our lives. You probably have some rules that you have followed for so long you haven't noticed them. Perhaps they are now habits or rituals you and your family follow. As you look closer at the role that rules have in not only our society but in your life, you'll find that rules free you up to live happliy, safely and comfortably within a framework created first in your imagination. You may also discover that some of the rules you've accepted without question are not working for you anymore. You may have inherited them from your parents or community or you may have outgrown them as your life has undergone its natural metamorphosis.

When you were a child, chances are your parents had rules for you about bedtime. The hour was spelled out and certain rituals observed such as brushing your teeth, reading for a short while and putting out the light. Now that you're an adult, you probably still do those same things in preparation for going to bed. But you may not have retained some of the other rules your parents had for you at that time such as wearing a retainer every night or not drinking any water for an hour before bed to keep from having an accident in the night. You outgrew those rules and they were no longer needed.

As you add to these rules below and on the next page, you may find that you're still clinging to some outdated rules. Write them down anyway because they add insight and understanding in your journey.

Sleeping
: In bed by 10, evening news, lights out by 11
Rise at 5 and read my email before I go to work.
No lights on in my room at night.

Exercise
: 15 mile bike ride every day.
Walk for half an hour every day.
Yoga every Friday at the Recreation Center.

Weight
: If I gain even 1 pound, no bread until I lose it
Weigh myself every morning

Public Appearance
: No sloppy clothes, even just to go to the corner store
Make-up! Always!

Food
: Leave a bite on my plate no matter what.
Sit down to eat.
No animal products whatsoever.
Everything must be raw.

Sex
: No sex on a first date.
Certain behaviors are completely unacceptable.

Housekeeping
: Dishes must be done before I go to bed.
Vacuum whole house every Saturday morning.

Exercise 10: Rules for the new You

In the previous exercises, you have essentially created a person that up until now did not *visibly* exist (you!). But for the purpose of this next exercise, I want you to pretend that this person you've defined is someone else. If you become mired down in your emotional response to making rules for yourself you may not create valid or honest rules.

You have this new person's picture (page 54) and you know their behavior, habits, and style. You know how it feels to be in their skin and look out at the world.

Start writing down rules on the next page referring to the definitions you provided in Exercises 6 and 7. Remember, you are defining this person (page 54) who lives life a certain way (pages 22 to 25).

A person who answered Exercise 6, Question 1 by saying that they get about 8 hours of sleep each night might have a rule that they go to bed by 10 pm and wake at 6 am.

You may find that you don't require rules for some of the lifestyle definitions. Don't be tempted to simply gloss over it. Write down at least one rule for each item in exercises 6 and 7. If you need more space, tape or staple paper right over the next page so you keep a record of this process.

Some example rules in certain areas have been given to you in the last exercise and you added some of your own rules, useful or obsolete, to that list.

When you're done writing down all the rules you can think up to support the answers in Exercises 6 and 7, you can go through and cross out the unimportant and obvious ones.

Only you can determine what sorts of rules you need to leave in to honor your true self. If your greatest personal imbalance is in the area of eating, you will want to keep a rule or rules for eating, and perhaps that will be where you want to focus right now. If the way in which you are not being true to your real self is in the way you dress, you might make a rule regarding your clothing.

Ten rules is a manageable number. In time, if those rules

work well for you, they will become habits and you can then add to or alter the rules to suit your evolving self.

    These are the rules for your true, inner self.

You may have certain challenges specific to your experiences or lifestyle that require you to formulate additional rules that are carved in stone and will never change. Examples might be if you have a substance abuse problem. I would recommend that you make a rule that you will not touch, consume, use – whatever – the substance you are challenged by, under any circumstances. I would suggest you go further and rule that you will not associate with (name names) or any other people who use/abuse/sell/whatever that substance. Make yourself such a strict set of rules regarding this that you will never find a loophole. And if you do find a loophole, identify it, fix it quickly, write it down and implement it immediately.

Addictions are so insidious that they masquerade as reason and logic while trying to entice you to engage in the addictive behavior. Cigarette smokers who quit report obsessive thoughts of having "just one puff" that felt perfectly reasonable while their bodies were in the withdrawl phase. Alcoholics often fall off the wagon with "just one drink."

Addictive behavior isn't always related to a substance. In recent years the press has disclosed stories of prominant people admitting to an addiction to sexual behavior and in my own practice I've counseled numerous women who were struggling with their husband's internet sex craving.

Beyond addictive behavior, their are other ways you might use the Carved in Stone rules. A person with herpes may limit sexual contact or declare they will always disclose their health status with any potential partners. Someone who struggles with taking things, could simply declare that she will never steal anything from anyone under any circumstance.

Often, just by making it a statement of fact, the person's view of herself changes.

Add your Carved in Stone rules to your list on page 55.

Section 4

Implementing your new rules for life

Begin as you mean to go on. And if you falter, begin again.

Implementing your new rules for life

Read your rules daily. Look at your definitions and pictures. Continue visualizing and defining yourself.

In our world today we have lots of rules, and many don't mean anything. The old adage "rules are meant to be broken" seems to have been embraced, adopted and is now the rule rather than the exception!

If you skipped ahead to this point, you're wondering how you're going to follow all these rules that seem arbitrary or meaningless. That's why the exercises that came before this point built you to an understanding, or even a passion to live the life of the real person you are. To be true to that person, you must live according to the pattern she or he is created under. Thin people eat like thin people. Smart people act like smart people. Successful people act like successful people. You will always find exceptions, but as far as you know, you may just be observing someone breaking their own rules, however briefly or publicly. So go forward under the assumption that whether the rules were defined for someone or by someone or by society, everything that anyone is or ever was operates within a set of rules.

Change the rules, and you change the situation. To change the situation, you must change the rules. It's simple.

Exercise 11: Challenges

Challenges – times/places where the rules will be hard to implement

Identify times when your rules might be hard to follow. Write the situation that might make it more of challenge to follow your rules on the first line and some strategies for handling and coping with the situation while staying true to your rule. The numbers refer to your list of rules.

Rule 1: _____

_____

_____

_____

Rule 2: _____

_____

_____

_____

Rule 3: _____

_____

_____

_____

Rule 4: _____

_____

_____

_____

Rule 5: _____

_____
_____
_____

Rule 6: _____

_____
_____
_____

Rule 7: _____

_____
_____
_____

Rule 8: _____

_____
_____
_____

Rule 9: _____

_____
_____
_____

Rule 10: _____

_____
_____
_____

Exercise 12: Rules for breaking your rules

We have a day of the week that we don't follow our food rules. That day is Sunday since we have, in years past, spent Sundays with our extended family. On those days we all would contribute to the feast of food and drink and many times there were foods that we weren't accustomed to eating put before us. I'm sure your mother told you the same thing my mother told me: you have to eat at least a few bites. So we tasted and tempted and often spent the rest of the day feeling rotten from over indulgence and the unusual foods all combined together. If someone was on a diet, they cheated. If someone ordinarily didn't eat sweets, they treated themselves.

For us it's natural that Sunday would be the day that we would eat whatever we liked. The only rule we have is that whatever we eat on Sunday must be eaten up or thrown out by Monday morning. At first, the kids chose extreme and excessive cheats. It only took a few weeks until they were ill from eating a gallon of ice cream and pounds of cheese along with huge containers of beef jerky. Last Sunday the cheat was a modest container of ice cream and a small block of cheese among 4 people. That was it!

We also allow ourselves to eat the common foods served during holiday feasts, or to consume what a hostess might serve. That sums up our rules for breaking our eating rules.

When you choose situations under which you will break your rules, they must be limited. You can't say, I will only smoke while out in a bar. You might find yourself hanging out at the corner tavern a lot! The rule exception must be very specific and very limited.

Sunday works for us because it's one day a week and is self-limiting. Holidays (Christmas, Thanksgiving, Easter and birthdays) are few and far between. But if your family is Jewish (lots of feast days) and there's 10 kids and 60 grandkids and everyone gets together for each birthday then this is *not* a good exception to your rule, or at the very least your exception might be that you will allow yourself 1 piece of birthday cake or one glass of wine or whatever, not carte blanche to tank up.

Suggestion: If you make rules that are contingent upon location, the location must be far, far away. *"When I'm on vacation more that 500 miles from home, I will allow myself to eat 1 steak dinner in a nice restaurant each week of my vacation."*

Suggestion: do not make rules that are contingent upon other people.

Your real self attracts people who fit into that personality. When you act like someone else, such as the person you've been hiding behind for all your life, you attract another sort of person. Those people are still valuable to you, and you will still care for them, but they are a reflection of a person who no longer exists. You can't use them as your exceptions because it would be very easy to slip back into that role. Additionally, one of the ways we acknowledge who we are is how we view the reflection of ourselves through the observations of others.

It might be valuable to look at your real self again (page 52) before you start chopping up your rules and deciding upon exceptions.

After each numbered rule, write down the circumstances that you will allow yourself an exception.

Rule 1: _____

Rule 2: _____

Rule 3: _____

Rule 4: _____

Rule 5: _____

Rule 6: _____

Rule 7: _____

Rule 8: _____

Rule 9: _____

Rule 10: _____

Exercise 13: Time for change (How to know when it's time to change your rules)

There may come a time when you realize that you have grown or changed in some way that requires you alter your rules for yourself. Maybe you find that your initial vision of yourself wasn't accurate or wasn't all that it was cracked up to be.

I had a vision of myself being a country person and living on the land. When I moved to the country I discovered that the things I loved about it were valid. I enjoyed gardening, and putting up the fruits of my labor by canning, drying and freezing. I loved the smells of farms and woods and a snow day thrilled me. I also discovered something else about myself that I never would have guessed; I love the city. I love the thrum of traffic and the availability of anything I want. I love museums and concerts and universities. I don't want to live there but I do want to live close enough to visit when I need a little culture. When I realized that, I refined my vision of myself. It now includes weekly trips to a large town for a meal or a glass of wine in a nice restaurant and a couple of hours in a large bookstore, and monthly trips to even larger metro areas. Nothing in those changes actually goes against my definition of me; I just subtly altered it to include some aspects of my personality I hadn't been aware of before.

Only you can know when it's time to change one of your rules, or how it needs to be changed. You might even want to make a rule that you won't change any of your rules more frequent than once a month. That way, you'll at least give each rule a chance.

Breaking a rule isn't a reason to get rid of it. A speed limit tells you how fast you're allowed to drive, but it often isn't followed. If you exceed the speed limit, and a police officer sees you, you run the risk of getting a ticket. That doesn't mean you now must always speed, or that the speed limit will change to reflect the miles per hour that drivers really travel. It means you broke the rule, you got caught, do better next time. That's the same way I hope you view the rules you've created here. If you break one, give yourself a mental ticket, then go back to following your rules. Don't treat the breaking of a rule as a reason to change it. You might break your rules 10 times or a hundred, but if you followed the exercises in this book, your reason for developing each rule was valid, and remains valid, even if you're having trouble following it.

This exercise is a long term one. Make notes as to how your vision is working for you and what you might change.

The rule for changing your rules is clear.
It is dependent upon your vision of yourself changing first.

When you change your rules, write them down in their new form and staple over the page of rules you have already defined in this book. Don't get rid of your old rules. You are building yourself, page by page, and your notes on those old rules are valuable and provide insight and awareness of who you are.

_____
_____
_____
_____
_____
_____
_____
_____
_____
_____
_____
_____
_____
_____
_____
_____
_____
_____
_____
_____

There is no ending

Defining ourselves is an ongoing investigation. Everyone has rules, though perhaps not written down. And some day, you may not need to have yours written down either. Until that day, keep this book close, refer to it often, build a case to be your authentic you, and enjoy your life.

Reference

List of descriptive words 46
Picture of your body with another face 48
Picture of your face on another body 49
Categorized people to study 50
Pictures of your role model 51
The "Real Me" in pictures 52
My Rules 53

List of Descriptive Words
Here are some words you might use:

active	conservative	goulish
angry	cool	grand
antagonistic	coordinated	gray
athletic	couch potato	green
auburn	cranky	gregarious
average	crowded	grubby
black	dark	happy
blonde	defensive	hazel
blue	dense	helpful
bohemian	drab	heterosexual
bossy	dyed	hippie
boy	earthy	homosexual
bright	energetic	hopeful
brown	exhausted	hopeless
brunette	extravagant	hot
bubbly	fake	hygienic
bulky	false	hyperactive
bully	fat	impaired
careful	female	impoverished
careless	feminine	intellectual
celibate	flabby	intelligent
cheesy	follower	intoxicated
childish	foolish	jumbo
chubby	funny	kind
chunky	fussy	large
clean	gay	lazy
clever	genius	leader
clumsy	girl	lesbian
cold	gleeful	liberal
colorful	goth	loser

loud
macho
male
man
masculine
mean
mediocre
melancholy
messy
meticulous
middle-aged
mismatched
muscular
naive
neat
nice
normal
obese
offensive
old
open
optimistic
ordinary
outgoing
over-done
overwhelmed
paranoid

passifist
peaceful
pessimistic
petite
plain
pleasant
plus-size
poor
preppy
pretentious
punk
quick
quiet
red
religious
rich
sad
salt and pepper
scowling
serious
sexy
shy
skinny
sleek
slim
small
smart

stinky
strange
strawberry blonde
strong
struggling
stupid
stylish
successful
super
svelte
thin
tiny
tired
troublesome
trusting
unhappy
uptight
warm
weak
wealthy
weird
white
winner
woman
yard sale
yellow
young

Your Body Picture

Your Face Picture

People
It used to be that young people had heroes, those people who stood for the traits, goals and ideals that a kid might hope to emulate. When you choose a person to pattern your life after, look at the whole person. We each are the sum of all our parts.

If you're stumped about who to pick to represent your ideals, this list might help. Obviously, I've categorized these people according to mine and others' observations, and they may not fit with yours at all. However, it should give you some ideas and help your brainstorming.

Artistic:
> Norman Rockwell (illustrator), Amy Brown (fantasy painter), Martha Stewart (home arts), Richard George Rogers (architect), J.K. Rowling (writer), Jim Henson (puppeteer). Hint: look up the type of artistic expression you favor and then see who are the top performers.

Intelligent:
> Bobby Fischer, Leonardo Da Vinci, Marilyn Vos Savant, Isaac Newton, Albert Einstein, Marie Curie, Stephen Hawkins

Athletic:
> Lance Armstrong, Babe Ruth, Tiger Woods, Serena Williams, Chris Evert

Successful in Business
> Donald Trump, Martha Stewart, Bill Gates, Sam Walton, Oprah, A.P. Giannini. Hint: Look up successful people by industry and other factors.

Inventor
> George de Mestral (*Velcro*), Steve Jobs (*Apple* computer), Ruth Handler (*Barbie* doll and later *Nearly Me*, a breast prosthesis for mastectomy patients), Earle Dickson (*Band-aid*)

Sexy
> Patrick Dempsey, Brad Pitt, Johnny Depp, Will Smith, Shemar Moore, Justin Timberlake, Angelina Jolie, Halle Berry, Jessica Simpson, Beyonce, Charlize Theron

Because of the nature of our society, many of these standards will change and so, too, will the people who represent them. You have your own standards that are more valid for you than Hollywood's.

Notes and/or Pictures

The real me

Rules

1. _____
2. _____
3. _____
4. _____
5. _____
6. _____
7. _____
8. _____
9. _____
10. _____

Carved in Stone

1. _____
2. _____
3. _____
4. _____
5. _____

www.ingramcontent.com/pod-product-compliance
Lightning Source LLC
Chambersburg PA
CBHW051716040426
42446CB00008B/918